No Skin
No Bone
No Fear.

MARTIN'S
FISHY FISHY
COOKBOOK

MARTIN'S
FISHY FISHY
COOKBOOK

MARTIN SHANAHAN

Photographs by Kevin O'Farrell

First published in April 2011
by Estragon Press, County Cork
© Estragon Press

Reprinted May 2011
Reprinted September 2011
Reprinted November 2012
Reprinted May 2014
Reprinted May 2015

Recipes © Martin Shanahan
Photographs © Kevin O'Farrell

The moral right of the author has been asserted

ISBN 978-1-906927-09-7

www.guides.ie

Acknowledgements

This book is dedicated to the fishermen of Ireland, who venture out in all weathers
and risk their lives to bring home to us the wonderful gift that is Irish seafood.

I would also like to thank Marie, Jack, Ben and Lucy for all their patience and support.

Thank you also to Sally, John and Kevin: without them there'd be no Fishy Fishy Cookbook.
To all the guys in RTE Cork, a big thank you for the wonderful experience I've had.
Thank you to Rory, Colm, Janet as well as Ben and Barry on camera, Brendan and
Kieran on sound, Deccie and Aoife and all the RTE crew back at the studio.
Thanks also to Mantis and Will, and to Dave and all the staff at Fishy Fishy.

Thanks to Ozzie and Ronnie, and to Maria and Jim, and to the
fishmongers of Ireland who work with our fish and shellfish.

And finally thanks to all our loyal customers who offer us the opportunity
to cook for them, and are always willing to try out new dishes.

Contents

Contents

Introduction

Food was a big part of growing up in Fermoy. My mom was a great cook, my gran was a great cook. We ate fish on Fridays, like everyone else; we had whiting, we had smoked fish with white sauce and onions and peas and mashed potatoes, which was gorgeous. I learnt to cook in Rockwell College, after I had finished school. I got the placing and thought I'd give it a shot. Then on my first summer placing out of Rockwell, I was sent to the Butler Arms in Waterville, County Kerry and this was great, because in comparison Rockwell was hard labour!

The Butler Arms was really built on the standard of its food, and people came for the food, which was all sourced locally. We had guys growing vegetables locally, and the meat and fish was all local, with a lot of guys turning up at the back door, with a load of lobsters, or crabs, and for me this was where it all fell into place.

My interest in cooking fish started there, because you had the quality, the freshness, the simplicity, and I saw how easy it was to cook. So I decided that if I was ever going to have my own place, I was going to cook seafood.

I worked in San Francisco at the end of the 1980's, and loved it. I loved how adventurous the people were, how multicultural it was, with a lot of Pacific Rim influences, especially with the fish cookery.

When we came back from San Francisco, we set up the original Kinsale Gourmet Store, a fish shop and a deli, and I learnt the fish business from the bottom up, which was great. I remember going to the fish auctions in Skibbereen, West Cork, and I had already planned in my head what I was going to buy and what I was going to do with it, and then arriving down at the auction hall to find that nothing that I had in my head was for sale on the floor! So I had to adapt fast. And after the first couple of trips you learnt how to improvise. It wasn't about picking up the phone and just getting fish from a wholesaler.

I also saw how many fish were underused and I thought, my God!, we should be selling ray wings, and haddock, and red gurnard. I learned the fish business inside out, I learned the seasons, I learned the supply and demand, and we discovered that when we started introducing the lesser-known fish, that people loved it. But that was simply because of the quality; always buying the best, freshest, seasonal fish. With fish, part of the fun of it is making connections, sourcing it from the guys, putting the extra effort into it. That's what we do.

I've always cooked by the sea, from the Butler Arms, to San Francisco, to Kinsale, it's always been by the water, and I just try to offer what people want to eat when they come to a coastal village like Kinsale. I remember many years ago Rick Stein turning up to Fishy Fishy to the original cafe and he just said this is what he wanted to find: a fish shop with a few tables where you can sit down and have a bowl of mussels, have a chowder, have some fish and chips. You want to find what is local, and what is local to the area.

We spent seven years as fish retailers in the Kinsale Gourmet Store, and I never really thought about going back into the restaurant business. But I was listening to customers, to tourists who were passing through, and they wanted to eat seafood in Kinsale but they couldn't get it: they wanted steamed mussels; they wanted fresh prawns, and they couldn't find them.

We needed to expand, and so in 1998 we moved around the corner to the Guardwell, where we had a fish shop and a deli, and we had a bit of room for about 20 seats. We did simple things — fish and chips; open prawn sandwiches, some specials, but what we also said was: if it's on the fish counter, but not on the menu, we will gladly cook it for you.

And it worked really well, and everything we seemed to try, people just loved. We put a little bit of a Californian twist on things and people went: wow! The success was a huge surprise, and after the first year it just went mad. But we just did what we wanted to do: cooking fresh fish in season, using the best product all the time, using my suppliers who work out of the port at Kinsale.

We opened the new Fishy Fishy in 2006 as we had simply outgrown the old building and needed more space. We have stuck with our ethos of local, fresh, seasonal fish, and of having a restaurant that is relaxed and informal, with great staff, staff who have real pride in their work, who get involved with the food because of its goodness.

Fish is nature's fast food. It comes from nature, and it's so fast and easy to cook. You can cook fish faster than you can cook a sausage, and if you can cook a sausage or a rasher, then you can cook fish. But for many people, there is a fear factor when it comes to cooking fish, and it means that many people believe they don't like fish. We knew from the minute we started retailing fish that if we skinned and boned the fish for our customers, that they would try it, and they would come back and say that it was lovely. You have to take out the 'fear factor': no skin, no bones, no fear.

Fish is a gift, it's not a commodity, and it deserves our respect. We have to respect its seasonality, and enjoy it. There are no secrets when it comes to cooking fish. You need to have a relationship with your fishmonger, you need to have a trust, and you need to ask them what is good. And if you can cook one type of fish, you can cook them all. You don't need fifty techniques. The varieties of fish are huge, but the techniques for cooking it are simple.

Fish is so intriguing, so fascinating, so colourful, even in its raw state. It's a chef's dream to cook fish, so you want to introduce it to everyone you can, and I love to have the opportunity to do that with people. There's a multitude of fish varieties, and just a couple of simple ways of cooking them to enjoy them at their best.

Martin Shanahan, Kinsale, March 2011

Fishy Fishy

SEAFOOD & OYSTER BAR
COCKTAIL & WINE BAR

Techniques

There are relatively few techniques involved when cooking fish, and consequently, if you master them then you will be able to cook literally any fish to perfection. Arm yourself with knowledge of how to pan-fry, oven-roast, steam and poach, and you can adapt any one of these techniques to all the different types of seafood. Remember, no skin, no bones, no fear.

Prawns

Remove the head, by twisting it off. It will come away easily. If you like, you can remove the black vein that runs along the back of the tail. If you look carefully at the tip of the tail you will see it is divided into three. Take the centre piece, twist gently to remove, and hopefully bring the centre vein with it.

Hold the tail in your two hands, twist gently, turning one hand clockwise, the other hand anti-clockwise. The shell of the prawn will split between your hands. Pull off the back and front sections of the shell carefully to reveal the whole prawn tail.

Skinning fish

Lay the fillet on a board and, holding the tail skin with one hand, slide a sharp knife underneath the fillet between it and the skin. Use a sawing action.

To skin a flat fish, start at the tip of the tail, score into the tail with a sharp knife and loosen a flap of skin. Pull hard on this skin, holding the fish in the other hand. The skin should peel off.

Opening an oyster

You will need an oyster knife and a cloth. Hold the oyster in the stiff cloth (to protect your hands) with the flatter shell uppermost. Find a gap between the upper and lower shell. Slide the knife blade parallel to the upper shell and sever the muscle attached to the oyster. Being careful not to lose any of the juices, force the top shell up to open the oyster. Remove the top shell.

Using the blade of the knife, separate the oyster from the lower shell. Tip out the juices into a jug (you might have to sieve them). Scrape away any fragments of shell from the oyster meat, which is now ready to serve or cook. Remember, if you are nervous about opening oysters, you can always ask your fishmonger to open them for you. Just make sure they keep the juice for you as well.

Preparing fresh crab

Place a large saucepan on the heat and add enough water to cover the crab. Warm the water. Put in the crab, and begin to turn up the heat. (Some people say this is easier for the crab, as it falls asleep. You may prefer to plunge the crab into boiling water, and get the process over more quickly.) Boil the crab for 15 to 20 minutes. Remove and cool completely — for at least 1 hour. Turn the cold crab over, remove the legs by pulling in the opposite direction from which they lie. Remove tail flap and discard. Next prise open the section, called the purse, to which all the legs were attached. An oyster knife is a good implement to do this with. Prise any white and brown meat from the purse, but discard the grey, feather-like fingers.

Press down the eye section of the crab, and pull away, lifting out the eyes and the stomach sac behind it. The shell contains the brown meat and the roe; spoon this out. The brown meat from inside the shell can then be processed in a food processor, after which it forms an absolutely delicious pâté-type mixture. To remove the white meat, smash the large front claws of the crab carefully, so as not to smash the meat. Pull away the flesh of the crab, including the meat that you will find in the pincers. The smaller legs don't have much meat in, and are best used as a garnish. When you have finished you will be left with a bowl of white meat and a bowl of brown meat. Use all the shells to make a stock or bisque (see page 42).

Cleaning and cooking mussels

If you have time, it's a good idea to put the mussels in a large bowl of fresh water, into which you have sprinkled a handful of oatmeal. The mussels take in the fresh water while eating the oatmeal, and it helps to get rid of any grit and impurities.

To cook: tip the mussels into a bowl and shake fairly aggressively until they all close (discard any that don't close). Rinse under fresh cold water. Drain. Put a large saucepan on the stove to heat and tip in the mussels. Cover and leave for a few minutes until the mussels open (discard any that don't open).

Thereafter, you can serve them straight away — a good accompaniment is the curry aioli on page 38. Or you can make a butter sauce by adding a glass of white wine or cider when cooking, along with two diced shallots, a handful of chopped parsley and a large knob of butter. When the mussels have opened, transfer them to a heated serving bowl. Strain the cooking liquid and boil it to reduce until thickened. Add another large chunk of butter, the juice of a lemon and some more parsley. Pour over the mussels and serve.

Preparing lobster

Cleaving a lobster is simple in comparison to preparing a crab. First cook the lobster in boiling water to cover for approximately 20 minutes. Allow to cool for an hour. If you are nervous about handling the live lobster, put it in the freezer for a couple of hours before cooking, at which point it will be comatose and simple to handle.

Place the cooked lobster on its stomach, detach the large claws. Insert the tip of a large kitchen knife into the point where the head shell meets the body shell. Press the knife down and cut through the tail. Turn the lobster 180° and cut through the head, leaving you with two equal halves of lobster. Remove the stomach sac, the gills (the grey feather-like fingers) and the black digestive tract. The brain has a plasticy texture, remove this too. Do not discard the pinky brown liver, known as the tomalley it is delicious.

How to buy fish

The sheer variety of fish and shellfish from Irish waters can seem utterly confounding when you walk into a fish shop. This is where your fishmonger's skill and expertise comes to the rescue. If you don't know what a particular fish is, never even mind how to cook it, then your fishmonger is there to make sure your dinner is going to be perfect. When you first cook fish the most reliable means to success is to ask for no skin and no bones. This means you can eat without fear of encountering a fish bone, which makes many people wary of cooking fish. As you get more experience you'll discover that the skin of many fish, as well as being particularly healthy, is also very delicious. When considering the bones, it is helpful to divide the main fish varieties into two groups. Flat fish, such as plaice, John Dory and brill have no pin bones, ie bones in the centre of the fish.

Because the bone is simple to deal with, these fish are often cooked and served whole and on the bone. The other main variety of fish is round fish. This group includes cod, salmon, hake and haddock. These fish have what is known as pin bones running through the top centre of the fillet, and these are the bones you want to have removed. Your fishmonger can remove these bones, either by removing them individually (pin boning), or by cutting a V shape in the top third of the fillet, removing all the bones along with some of the flesh. Next we come to skin. You can ask the fishmonger to skin the fillet for you, and my preference is to remove the skin from hake, haddock, cod, white pollock and gurnard. I prefer to leave the skin on with salmon and mackerel, because it cooks deliciously crispy. Most fishmongers leave the skin on flat fish such as plaice and sole, but don't be afraid to ask them to remove it.

Roasting fish

Roasting suits both whole fish and fish fillets. Preheat your oven to its highest setting, at least 200°C. Put a frying pan on the hob, over a high heat. You will need a frying pan that can also be put in the oven. (Otherwise you can use a hob-proof baking dish, such as a Le Creuset dish.)

When the pan is very hot, place some oil in the pan (I often use an ordinary vegetable oil, or an olive oil. Pure Irish rapeseed oil is also fantastic for cooking fish because it holds the heat very well.) Place your fish, presentation side up, into the hot pan. Cook for a couple of minutes, and then lift the whole pan off the stove and place into the oven for a further 5 — 10 minutes, depending on the thickness of the fish.

You can also carry out the whole process on a roasting tray. Preheat your oven, and place the tray in the oven to heat. It's a good idea to score the fish for this method of cooking, because it helps to cook the fish more evenly. Make three cuts through the skin and into the flesh of the fish (you can insert herbs into these cuts for added flavour). When the tray is very hot, remove from the oven and, working quickly, sprinkle the tray with oil. Holding the fish by the tail 'wash it' in the oil so it is lightly coated on both sides, place on the hot tray, and place back into the oven. The heat of the tray will cook the fish from the underside as the top of the fish cooks.

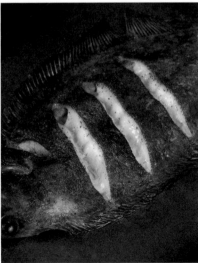

Steamed or poached fish or shellfish

Fish bouillon
500ml water
½ cup white wine vinegar
2 bay leaves
salt and 10 cracked peppercorns
the juice of 1 lemon
fresh parsley

Steaming and poaching are suitable for whole fish, such as whole salmon, as well as for precooking fish that might be used in a crumble or casserole.

For steaming fish, use salted water, and for poaching fish, use a bouillon. Poached fish should be simmered, never boiled, while shellfish can be cooked very quickly at a gentle bubble.

To make the bouillon, place all the ingredients in a large saucepan, and bring to the boil. Simmer for 10 minutes to infuse the flavours. Strain and use for poaching fish.

If you have a fish poacher, then this is especially suitable for large fish, otherwise small fish, as well as fish steaks and fillets of fish, can be steamed in any steamer that will accommodate them.

If you are poaching fish for a number of people, try poaching it in the oven. Pour the water into a deep roasting tray, add vinegar, lemon, peppercorns, bay leaves and parsley and place in a 200°C oven to heat. When the liquid is hot add the fish and poach for approximately 10 minutes, or until the fish is cooked. Cooking in the oven will ensure the water never boils and the fish will cook evenly.

Panfried fish

Pan frying is suitable for all types of white fish fillets. You can pan fry with the skin on — which is a technique especially suited for fish without scales, such as John Dory. Oily fish fillets, such as salmon and mackerel suit this type of cooking too, but there is no need to flour the oily fish when frying. (Note coeliacs needn't use flour, just keep the heat very high.) Make sure to use a heavy-based pan, this is essential. A light pan will smoke at high temperatures, and turning the heat down will cause your fish to stick.

Technique for white fish

Put a dry frying pan onto the heat, and leave it to heat up. Dry the fish and then dip into seasoned flour, shaking off any excess. Pour some oil into the pan, and place the fish, presentation side down. You might wish to serve the fish with a crispy skin, facing up, in which case cook the skin side first, or you might have skinned your fish beforehand. Whichever you choose, cook the side you want to see facing you on the plate first.

Cook for approximately four minutes, keeping the heat very high, with timing depending on the thickness of your fish. Turn the fish over, and cook on the other side. At this stage I often add a knob of butter or a sprinkling of water, if I think the pan is getting too dry. Cook for a further three to four minutes.

Technique for oily fish

Mackerel is very good when pan fried with its skin on, and salmon suits pan frying too. The secret here is heat, and not shaking the pan. Heat your pan until it is blazing hot. Add some oil. Season your fish but don't flour. Cook the fish presentation side first on the blazing heat, you must hear it sizzle. Don't be tempted to move the fish about. Turn after four minutes, by which time it will have a lovely crispy seal.

Basics

Irish soda bread, I think more than any other loaf, compliments good fish cookery and this is a simple recipe for a loaf that we cook every day. And here are some of the building blocks to great fish cooking.

Brown soda bread

butter or oil to grease 900g loaf tin
450g wholewheat flour
1 tablespoon wheatgerm
1 tablespoon bran
pinch of salt
½ tablespoon bread soda
600ml buttermilk

Preheat the oven to 175°C. Grease or butter a 900g loaf tin. You can also use a tin liner (available from kitchen shops). Measure the flour into the bowl, and add the wheatgerm, bran, and salt. Sift in the bread soda. Finally stir in the buttermilk, mixing with a wooden spoon until everything is combined. Place in a greased loaf tin. The dough should reach almost to the top of the tin. Bake in the preheated oven for 50 minutes.

Take out of the oven and let rest on a wire rack until cool. This bread is best served on the day it is made.

Fish stock

heads and bones of 1½kg flat fish
1 carrot, scrubbed and chopped roughly
1 onion, peeled and halved
1 stalk celery, chopped
2 bay leaves
10 crushed black peppercorns
3 litres water

Put all the ingredients into a large saucepan, and bring to the boil. Skim the surface of the foam that will gather, and then simmer for absolutely no more than 15 minutes. Strain.

Flavoured mayonnaise

Cocktail sauce

200ml mayonnaise

50ml tomato ketchup

1 tablespoon worcestershire sauce

1 teaspoon tabasco

1 tablespoon grated horseradish

Tartare sauce

100ml mayonnaise

2 anchovies

1 tablespoon capers, chopped

4 gherkins, chopped

generous handful fresh parsley, chopped

Tarragon and orange mayonnaise

100ml mayonnaise

1 tablespoon tarragon vinegar

grated zest of 1 orange

juice of ½ an orange

salt and pepper

1 tablespoon finely chopped fresh tarragon

Rocket mayonnaise

100ml mayonnaise

60g rocket

juice of ½ lemon

Lime and lemon mayonnaise

100ml mayonnaise

juice of 1 lemon

juice of 2 limes

Curry aïoli

100ml mayonnaise

1 teaspoon lemon juice

1 tablespoon curry paste

1 clove garlic, finely minced

Wasabi mayonnaise

100ml mayonnaise

2 — 3 tablespoons wasabi paste

salt and pepper

Simply combine the ingredients to flavour each mayonnaise. For the rocket mayonnaise you will need to combine in a food processor.

Shellfish

Shellfish are good for you, and they are easy to prepare. In Ireland we are blessed with the best shellfish, especially our lovely prawns — don't buy imports.

I recommend you always buy shellfish from a good fishmonger, don't be tempted to pick them on the beach! Shellfish bought from a fishmonger, even if caught in the wild, will have already been purified. If you buy uncooked lobster or crab — make sure it's still alive when you buy it.

Shellfish all have their own seasons, your fishmonger will be more than happy to guide you, and, because shellfish is a delicate product, it is a good idea to contact your fishmonger in advance and order it specially. Give a ring the day before.

Crab bisque

Serves 6

1 crab, cooked
2 onions
3 carrots
3 stalks of celery
peppercorns
bay leaf
olive oil
2 litres water
dash brandy
4 tablespoons tomato purée
150ml cream, plus a little whipped cream for serving

Cook and crack open the crab (see page 26). Place the brown meat in a small container or liquidiser and buzz to a purée. Reserve the white meat for garnish.

Pre-heat the oven to its maximum setting. Peel and roughly dice the onions, carrots and celery and place on a roasting tray with the peppercorns and bay leaf. Place the crab shells on top and drizzle over some olive oil. Roast in the oven for half an hour until the vegetables begin to caramelise.

Put the crab shell mixture into a large saucepan and add the tomato purée and water (use a little water to scrape everything from the roasting dish). Bring to the boil and simmer for an hour.

Strain the mixture. Discard the crab bits and vegetables. Put the stock back on to boil and boil hard until the mixture has reduced by about two thirds. Add the brandy and cream. When you are ready to serve the soup, stir in the puréed brown crab meat. Reheat and serve garnished with a little of the white crab meat and a little more whipped cream.

To make a crab butter
When you have made the stock, reserve three ladlefuls of liquid. Reduce this to a thick purée and mix with 75g of butter to make a crab butter. Wrap and chill the butter and cut into coins — lovely over fillets of fish. Note, this freezes well.

This is a great way to use every bit of the crab. However hard you might try to remove it, there is always a hidden wealth of meat secreted in the various crevices and extremities of a crab, and they make this a delicious, invigorating soup which is thickened with the brown meat.

Potato, leek and mussel soup

Serves 8 — 10

1 onion
200g leeks
1kg potatoes
1 tablespoon oil
salt
white pepper
2 litres water
100ml cream
1kg mussels in their shells
chives and sour cream for garnish

Peel and slice the onion, leeks and potatoes. Heat a tablespoon of oil in a medium saucepan and sweat the onion and leeks. Season with a little salt and pepper. Add the sliced potatoes.

Pour over the water and bring to the boil. Simmer for 20 minutes until the potatoes are soft. Blend the ingredients to a purée and add the cream.

Beard and wash the mussels. Steam in a little water until opened and cooked. Don't use mussels that don't open. Add the cooking juices from the mussels to the soup.

Remove the mussel meat from the shells and fold into the soup. Taste and season. Leave a few mussels in their shells for a garnish, and serve the soup with sour cream and chives.

This makes a fine, big pot of soup, suitable for 8 — 10 people. Make the soup in advance and then add the mussels just before serving.

Red chowder

Serves 6

1 tablespoon cooking oil
400g prawn heads
200g carrots, scrubbed and chopped
200g onions, peeled and chopped
3 sticks celery, sliced
4 tablespoons tomato purée
2 litres water
2 cloves garlic, sliced
1 tablespoon dried French tarragon
1 tablespoon ground coriander
1 tablespoon olive oil

375g diced fish chowder mix and a few peeled prawn tails
170ml carton cream
50g butter, softened
50g flour
cream to serve

Heat a large saucepan and add the oil. Cook the prawn heads and prepared vegetables in the pan over a high heat, crushing the prawn shells as you cook. Add the tomato purée and the water. Simmer for about 30 minutes and then strain. Add the garlic, coriander and tarragon.

Make a paste with 50g soft butter, and 50g flour. Spoon a little of the hot prawn stock into the paste, stirring to mix. Pour this paste back into the hot prawn stock, stirring over the heat at the same time, and continue to stir until you get a thickened stock. Season and simmer for half an hour to cook out the flour. Add the chowder mix and cream and serve. I like to garnish it with some fresh crab meat, cream and parsley oil, but a dollop of cream will suffice.

There are thousands of variations of chowders around Ireland. I think it's a very personal dish, with each chef using his own creativity. No two chowders are ever the same, and this is my version.

Steamed prawns with garlic, parsley and lemon

2 tablespoons water
8 — 10 prawns per person
3 cloves garlic
50g butter
juice of half a lemon
flat leaf parsley, chopped
crusty bread to serve

Put a pan on the heat and add the water. Put the prawns into the pan and steam for about 2 — 3 minutes with the lid on.

Peel and slice the garlic. Add the garlic to the pan, and then the butter and lemon juice, and finally the chopped parsley.

Serve immediately with crusty bread.

They're called prawns not langoustines! Also known as Dublin Bay prawns these are so much purer, tastier and ecologically better than imported tiger prawns. This is nature's fast food. The prawns need very little seasoning, and always add the herbs at the last minute to preserve their colour.

Fritto misto

Seafood mixture including
Mussels in their shells
oysters
squid
scallops
monkfish
plaice
salmon
sprat
sardines

Vegetable mixture including
broccoli, par boiled, but still crisp
courgette
sweet potato
baby corn
carrots

flour, seasoned with salt and pepper
oil for deep frying

Fritto misto sauce
4 gherkins
handful chives
handful fresh parsley
200ml mayonnaise
2 tablespoons capers
juice of half a lemon
lemon wedges to serve

Steam the mussels, drain, and leave them in their shells. Open the oysters and remove from the shell. Clean the squid, reserve the tentacles, and slice the main body of the squid in half lengthways. Score the inside of the squid in a criss cross pattern, and slice. Slice the scallops and their coral in half, widthways. Skin, bone and fillet the white fish and salmon, and slice into even slices, all the same size. Your fishmonger would be more than happy to do this for you.

Peel and chop all the vegetables into equal finger-sized-batons (there is no need to peel the sweet potato, just scrub it).

To make the sauce: finely dice the gherkins, snip the chives and parsley and stir all the sauce ingredients into the mayo. Squeeze in the lemon juice and then mix.

When you are ready to serve the fritto misto, heat the oil to 190°. Toss the vegetables and fish in the seasoned flour. Deep fry in batches. The fish and vegetables will cook in a couple of minutes and the shellfish in less than a minute. Serve garnished with the sauce and lots of lemon wedges.

This makes a great alternative to a summer barbecue. Get a long extension lead and take your deep-fat fryer into the garden. Have everything ready, including the sauce, then fry the food and watch it get devoured.

Hot oysters in coconut milk

1 chilli
200ml coconut milk
1 blade of lemon grass
2 limes
handful of coriander
6 oysters

Slice the chilli finely. Heat the coconut milk. Add the lemon grass and chilli. Squeeze the juice of one lime and add to the milk. Turn up the heat and simmer to reduce and thicken the sauce. Open the oysters (you can ask your fishmonger to do this, of course) and add to the sauce. Cook for two minutes.

Then, chop the coriander and stir into the sauce. Carefully place the oysters back into their shells, arrange on a plate and drizzle over some of the sauce. Squeeze some more lime juice over and serve.

I like to serve oysters on some bladderwrack seaweed, which we collect from the beach. We boil the seaweed until it goes bright green. You can't eat it, but it makes a lovely base for shellfish on the plate.

Lobster spring rolls

Makes approximately 15 spring rolls

1 uncooked lobster (about 500 – 600g)
1 carrot
half a head of Chinese cabbage
1 red pepper
1 yellow pepper
1 leek
the juice of 1 lime
1 tablespoon sesame oil
1 tablespoon light soy sauce
flour to make a paste
spring roll wrappers
oil for deep frying

Dipping sauce

1 tablespoon sugar
50ml rice vinegar
juice of 1 lime
1 tablespoon fish sauce
3 shallots, very finely diced
1 chilli, very finely diced

Prepare the lobster according to page 28. Wash the knife and cut all the meat into slivers.

Peel and grate the carrot into a bowl. Finely slice the cabbage, peppers and leek and add to the carrot. Add the lime juice, sesame oil and soy sauce and toss very lightly, so the mixture stays soft and loose. Add the lobster meat to the salad and toss very carefully to combine.

Make a paste with some flour and a little water. Place a spring roll wrapper on to a board. Spoon a heaped table-spoon of the filling in the centre. Pull a triangle of the wrapper over, and do the same on the opposite side. Then roll up from the side, using a little paste to seal the wrap when you reach the end. Repeat until all the filling is used up.

To make the dipping sauce, dissolve the sugar in the rice vinegar and then add all the rest of the sauce ingredients.

Heat the oil to 170°. Carefully place the spring rolls into the oil and cook, 4 at a time for about 2 – 3 minutes. Serve while hot, accompanied by the dipping sauce.

I like to serve lobster this way for a buffet party. It's tasty and fun, and quite economical. After making the rolls, roast the empty head and shell of the lobster to make either a lobster stock, or a bisque following the same recipe as the crab bisque on page 42.

Prawns with ginger, spring onions and sweet chilli

For each serving

6 uncooked whole prawns
25g butter
1 tablespoon sweet chilli sauce
juice of half a lime
half a tablespoon of pickled ginger, cut into julienne strips
2 spring onions, thinly sliced
bunch of coriander leaves

Remove the heads from the prawns, but don't shell them. Put a frying pan containing a few tablespoons of water on to the heat. Add the prawns and cook with the lid on for 1 — 2 minutes, until they colour. Add the butter, the chilli sauce and lime juice, and then finish with the pickled ginger, spring onions and chopped coriander.

To me, this is the seafood version of chicken wings, or spare ribs. Tasty finger food.

Crab cakes

Makes 6 cakes

2 stalks of celery
1 red pepper
olive oil
250g white crab meat
325g mashed potato
salt and pepper
flour, seasoned with salt and pepper
1 egg, beaten
white breadcrumbs
knob of butter

String and chop the celery, deseed and finely dice the red pepper. Heat a pan, add the olive oil, and sweat the celery and pepper for a couple of minutes until just soft.

Combine the crab meat, celery and pepper, mashed potato and seasoning. Mix together, using your hands, so as not to break up the crab meat.

Wet your hands, then form into cakes — this amount of crab and potato should make six good-sized cakes. Another way of doing this is to use an ice cream scoop. Scoop out portions of the mixture and then flatten with your hand.

Dip the cakes into seasoned flour, then dip into the beaten egg and finally the breadcrumbs. Leave in the fridge to cool for about 20 minutes, and then cook exactly as you would a piece of fish, in a hot pan with some oil. Cook for about 3 minutes, turn and add a little butter, before cooking for a further 3 minutes.

Serve these crab cakes with a little of the tomato relish from page 175 and some fresh rocket.

Grilled scallops in their shell with anchovy and lime butter

Serves 4

12 scallops
vegetable oil for cooking

Anchovy and lime butter
6 fillets of canned anchovy
the juice of half a lime
125g butter

Serve this with some crusty bread to mop up the buttery juices.

To make the butter: using a pestle and mortar, blend the anchovies with the lime juice, and then blend in the butter. Turn the grill on to maximum. Brush the scallops and four scallop shells with oil, and place the scallops back inside — placing three scallops to each half shell.

Grill for 1 — 2 minutes on each side. Serve with a dollop of the flavoured butter spooned into each shell.

Calamari with rocket mayonnaise

For each serving

1 baby squid, or half a large squid
quarter cup of flour
salt and pepper
1 tablespoon paprika
oil for deep frying
mixed green salad leaves
lemon wedges

Rocket mayonnaise
200ml mayonnaise
60g rocket
juice of half a lemon

To make the mayonnaise, place the rocket and lemon juice in a blender, whizz for about 30 seconds to make a purée, and then add the mayonnaise. Blend again until you get a smooth green sauce.

To make the calamari: mix together the flour, salt, pepper and paprika. Dry the squid on kitchen paper, and then coat in the seasoned flour. Deep fry in oil at 170°C for 2 minutes, until crisp.

To serve, place on plates with lemon wedges and some rocket mayonnaise.

Barbecued prawns in their shell

For each serving

8 whole prawns in their shell
3 tablespoons olive oil
80mls vegetable oil
handful of fresh herbs (could be parsley, basil, rocket, coriander or chervil)
1 clove garlic
juice of half a lemon
lemon wedges

Make a herb oil by blending the herbs with a tablespoon of the vegetable oil, then add the remaining oil and blend again.

Leave the heads on the prawns, but split the tail section in half lengthways with a sharp knife. Place in a bowl with a little of the herb oil and the sliced garlic. Toss to coat the prawns.

When you are ready to serve the prawns cook for about 2 minutes each side on a hot barbecue or grill. Put on a platter and serve drizzled with the rest of the herb oil and some lemon wedges.

Cooking prawns in their shell on a barbecue or under a grill gives them some protection from the heat, and makes for great finger food as part of a seafood barbecue. There's flavour in every part of the prawn.

Squid with chorizo

Serves 2

Balsamic glaze
1 cup aged balsamic vinegar (3 − 5 year old)
¼ cup sugar

300g squid
1 fresh chorizo, diced
wild rocket

Put the balsamic vinegar and sugar in a small saucepan and boil until it has reduced by half.

Cut the squid lengthways and score the inside with a sharp knife, cutting a little way through the surface, but not right through. Then dice the squid into pieces about 2½ cm square.

Pan fry the squid and the diced chorizo over a high heat for about a minute before putting on the plate and topping with some wild rocket. Drizzle over some of of the balsamic glaze.

Scoring the squid on the inside will tenderise the meat. Cook this dish quickly over a very high heat.

Shrimp omelette

Per person

juice of half a lemon
handful of salt
handful of uncooked shrimps
3 eggs
cooking oil

Bring a small pan of water to the boil and add the lemon juice and salt. Add the shrimps to the pan and simmer for about one and a half minutes — they should change colour. Drain, cool and peel the shrimps.

Beat the eggs together in a bowl with a pinch of salt. Place an omelette pan on the heat and add a little bit of oil. Pour the eggs into the pan, and as the egg begins to set, pull in the edges and let the liquid egg fall into the base of the hot pan. When the egg is almost cooked sprinkle on the cooked and peeled shrimps. Fold over and serve immediately. The whole process takes less than a minute to cook.

I came up with this recipe for my local shrimp fishermen. It's something they can easily cook on board. On the boat, the shrimp would probably be cooked in sea water. Get the same effect at home by using heavily salted water.

Scallop with black pudding and parsnip purée

Serves 2

2 parsnips
pinch of grated nutmeg
1 teaspoon honey, plus a little more for the glaze
knob of butter (approximately 20g)
cream (approximately 1 tablespoon)
oil
4 slices of black pudding
juice of half a lemon
rosemary

Peel the parsnips and roughly chop. Cook in a little boiling water until soft. Strain, add the nutmeg and honey, a few knobs of butter and a drop of cream. Mash with a potato masher, or purée with a hand-held liquidiser.

Sauté the black pudding in a little oil, on both sides, over medium heat for about two minutes per side. Put a separate pan on a high heat, add a little oil. Add the scallops. Cook for two minutes, making sure not to disturb the scallops whilst cooking, you want to achieve a caramelised crust. Remove the scallops from the pan, add a spoon of honey, and some lemon juice to make a glaze.

Assemble the dish by putting a little parsnip mash in the centre, topping with alternate slices of pudding and scallop, pouring over the glaze, and garnish with a little fresh rosemary.

This makes an unusual first course. Scallops need very little preparation — but there is a little tight muscle on one side, which you can remove with a sharp knife. Scallops have a wonderful affinity with Irish artisan black pudding.

Spaghetti with prawns

Serves 4

500g peeled prawn tails
450g spaghetti
2 heads of broccoli, separated into florets
olive oil for frying
4 cloves garlic, peeled and sliced
200ml cream
knob of butter
salt and pepper
Parmesan cheese, grated

Cook the spaghetti in boiling salted water. Cut the broccoli into small florets and cook in boiling salted water for approximately 3 — 4 minutes, then drain.

Heat a large pan and add the oil. Sauté the prawns for approximately 30 seconds. Remove and set aside. Heat the pan again, and this time add the sliced garlic and the cream. Bring to the boil to reduce slightly, and season with salt and pepper, and add a knob of butter. Add the broccoli to the cream, and then gently stir in the prawns. Add the cooked, drained spaghetti and toss. Serve with freshly grated Parmesan.

You can use fresh or frozen prawns with this recipe, but make sure to use Irish prawns.
Kids just love all the zappy, in-your-face flavours of this dish.

Crab risotto

1 whole crab, including white and brown meat
1 small butternut squash
vegetable oil
salt
1 onion
300g risotto rice
1 litre chicken or vegetable stock
25g butter
50ml cream

Preheat your oven to 180°C for roasting the squash.

Cook and crack open the crab (see page 26). Place the brown meat into a small container or liquidiser and buzz to a purée. Both white and brown meat will be used in the risotto.

Peel the butternut squash, remove the seeds and dice the flesh into small cubes. Place the squash onto a roasting tray and drizzle generously with the oil. Season with salt and roast in the oven for 10 — 12 minutes.

To make the risotto: finely dice the onion, heat 2 table-spoons of olive oil and cook the onion over medium heat until softened. Add the risotto rice, and stir to coat with the oil. Heat the stock and begin ladling it into the risotto, over medium heat, stirring between each ladleful until the liquid has been absorbed, before adding the next ladleful. The whole process takes around 20 minutes.

When the risotto is cooked, gently stir in the roasted squash and the brown crab meat. Add the butter and cream and serve, garnished with the white crab meat.

If you buy an uncooked crab, make sure it is alive when you buy it. Alternatively use a cooked whole crab, which are now widely available. Using the brown crab meat gives the risotto great depth of flavour.

Crab crumble

Serves 4 — 6

Lemon butter sauce
500ml cream
100g butter
juice of 2 lemons
salt and white pepper

4 tablespoons chopped parsley
50ml olive oil
100g breadcrumbs
400g white crab meat

Preheat the oven to 200°C.

To make the lemon butter sauce, place all the sauce ingredients in a small saucepan and bring to the boil. Simmer until it reduces slightly. Purée the parsley in the olive oil to make a parsley oil and mix this with the breadcrumbs.

When you are nearly ready to serve the crumble, divide the crab meat between four to six single serving oven-proof dishes. Pour some lemon butter sauce over each one and scatter liberally with the breadcrumb mixture.

Cook the crumbles in the oven for 5 — 6 minutes, or until the breadcrumbs are crispy.

All of these ingredients can be prepared ahead and just put together and cooked at the last minute.

Fishy fishy crab cocktail

Serves 4

1 recipe tomato salsa (see page 175)
shredded lettuce
375 g white crab meat

Cocktail sauce
200ml mayonnaise
75ml tomato ketchup
1 tablespoon Worcestershire sauce
1 teaspoon Tabasco
1 tablespoon grated horseradish

crab claws (for decoration)
brown crab meat (optional)

Mix the ingredients for the cocktail sauce together in a small bowl.

Take four individual serving glasses or bowls and fill each base with some tomato salsa. Next, add a layer of shredded lettuce. Then top with the white crab meat. Drizzle over some cocktail sauce and garnish with a crab claw and a little more lettuce.

If you have brown crab meat, you can serve this in a small ramekin dish, alongside.

In Fishy Fishy Café this crab cocktail is served in tall, slender glasses.

Avocado with fresh prawns

Serves 1

1 ripe avocado
10 fresh prawns
sprig of parsley
slice of lemon

Cocktail sauce
200ml mayonnaise
75ml tomato ketchup
1 tablespoon worcestershire sauce
1 teaspoon tabasco
1 tablespoon grated horseradish

Prepare the prawns according to page 25. Bring a small saucepan of water to the boil, add the lemon juice and parsley and salt. Add the prawns and simmer for two minutes. Drain and cool.

Slice the avocado in half and remove the centre stone. Carefully balance the prawns to make a little hill of seafood on top of each avocado half. Coat with the cocktail sauce and garnish with the parsley and lemon.

Fresh prawns and avocado are like strawberries and cream. They're made for each other, a classic recipe that never dates.

Oily fish

The omega rich food of all time — make oily fish a regular part of your diet, and here are some great ways to serve them.

Grilled salmon with home fries and fried egg

For each serving

vegetable oil
1 potato, cooked and diced
1 spring onion, sliced
2 slices smoked salmon
1 tablespoon horseradish sauce
lemon juice
1 egg
parsley to garnish

Preheat your grill to its maximum temperature.

Heat a pan on the hob and add the vegetable oil. Toss the potato in the hot oil until browned, then add a little sliced spring onion.

Rub a tray with oil and place the salmon on top. Rub some horseradish sauce on the salmon and squeeze lemon juice over. Place under the grill and cook for about 2 minutes.

Heat a pan to medium, add a good amount of oil and fry the egg.

Arrange the cooked potato on a plate, put the salmon on top and then place the fried egg on top of that. Garnish with a sprig of parsley.

When frying an egg use plenty of oil, then it cooks quickly and evenly. This is my Fishy Fishy version of the great Irish breakfast.

Warm smoked mackerel salad

1 whole mackerel, smoked
125g vine tomatoes
100g cucumber
half a red onion
salt
1 generous tablespoon sherry vinegar
handful of rocket leaves, washed
crusty bread

Heat your oven to 180°C.

First prepare the mackerel. Remove the head, and peel off the skin. Carefully remove the two fillets, using a sharp knife.

Oil a roasting pan and place the mackerel fillets onto the pan. Place the fish in the oven for 5 minutes just to warm through and release the juices and oils.

Make the salad while the fish is warming. Chop the tomatoes, cube the cucumber (leave the skin on), and dice the red onion finely. Season with salt and add the sherry vinegar. Toss the salad.

Take two serving plates and share the salad between the two plates, spooning onto the centre of the plate. Place the mackerel fillets on top, and then scrape the juices and oil from the tray on top of the salad as well. Top with a handful of rocket, and serve with warm crusty bread.

I like to think of mackerel as the rasher of the sea; you can do so much with it. It can stand on its own, or it works in the background. It's great for breakfast, and one of my favourite ways of serving it is in this warm salad, where the oils and smoky juices combine with sherry vinegar to make a simply smashing salad.

If you like, you can use mackerel fillets to make this salad, but I prefer to buy mackerel that has been smoked whole. When smoked like this the mackerel is hung by the gills during the smoking process, rather than being smoked flat on trays. This method gives the flesh a moist texture, and a lovely white colour.

Pan-fried mackerel with simple tomato sauce

Serves 4

4 canned plum tomatoes or ripe fresh tomatoes
2 cloves garlic
butter
bunch of flat-leaf parsley
salt and pepper
vegetable oil
4 mackerel, filleted and boned, but not skinned

Roughly chop the tomatoes, and the garlic. Melt the butter in a saucepan, add the plum tomatoes. Cook for a minute and then add the garlic, toss, and finally add some flat-leaf parsley.

Season the mackerel with the salt and pepper. Heat a heavy pan for five minutes, then add the oil. Cook mackerel in the hot oil, skin side down. For the first part of the cooking time, press the fish down with a spatula so that the skin crisps. Turn over and cook for a couple of minutes on the other side.

Place two fillets per person on a plate and spoon over some sauce.

When cooking skin-on mackerel, begin the process on the skin side and press the fish with a spatula against the hot pan. This will crisp the skin to perfection.

Grilled mackerel with honey and soy dressing

Serves 4

handful black and white sesame seeds
4 whole mackerel
olive oil

Honey and soy dressing
100ml soy sauce
100ml toasted sesame oil
50ml white wine vinegar
100ml honey
half a clove garlic, minced

Put the sesame seeds into a dry pan and place over the heat. Stir frequently while they toast. Don't leave them, as they will burn quickly.

The mackerel should be gutted and cleaned, but left whole. Score the skin with a sharp knife. Brush lightly with olive oil. Cook under a hot grill for 8 minutes, turning after 4 minutes. Mix together the dressing ingredients. Plate the cooked fish and drizzle over the dressing. You can serve extra dressing in a jug. Garnish with toasted black and white sesame seeds.

This recipe is ideal for the mackerel you might catch yourself in the summer. Just gut them (out at sea if possible), and clean them. They are left whole, with both head and tail on. You can cook them inside on a grill, or outside on a barbecue.

Mackerel with warm potato and chorizo salad

Serves 4

600g potatoes, cooked
1 fresh chorizo sausage (approximately 65g)
oil
200g green beans, cooked
8 mackerel fillets

Vinaigrette
1 tablespoon red wine vinegar
1 teaspoon French mustard
3 tablespoons olive oil
salt and pepper

Cube the cooked potatoes and slice the sausage. Heat a little bit of oil in a pan and add the chorizo, cook for a minute or two to release the oil from the sausage and then add the potatoes and the green beans. Make your vinaigrette by combining the vinaigrette ingredients and toss the potato mixture in this dressing.

Heat a pan over a high heat and add a little oil. Cook the mackerel skin side down, pressing down on the skin to crisp it. Cook for two minutes and then turn and cook for a further two minutes on the other side.

Spoon a little of the warm potato salad into the centre of each plate, and top with the mackerel fillets.

You can substitute a little lightly cooked kale for the green beans in this recipe, if preferred. In the restaurant I use the fresh West Cork chorizo from Gubbeen Smokehouse.

Seatrout with peas and new potatoes

Serves 4

700g new potatoes
300g peas (fresh or frozen)
60g butter
pinch of sugar
salt and pepper
fresh mint, chopped
4 fillets of sea trout
oil for cooking

Wash and cook the potatoes, then drain.

While the potatoes are cooking put the peas in a pan, add a few tablespoons of water, the butter and a little sugar. Cook the peas for a few minutes, and then season with salt and pepper and the chopped mint.

Season the fish. Put a pan on the heat and add some oil when it is hot. Place the sea trout into the very hot pan and leave, untouched for two minutes, so that the surface of the trout gets crunchy and crispy. Turn over and cook a further 2 — 3 minutes.

Serve the sea trout with the potatoes and peas.

This dish always reminds me of the start of summer. Look for organic farmed sea trout, which, for me, is the closest thing we can get nowadays to wild salmon. It's full of flavour as well as being very good for you.

Chicken of the sea with spinach

Serves 6

200g salmon
150g white fish (ling, cod, pollock, whiting)
1 egg
sprig of tarragon, shredded
salt and pepper
juice of 1 lemon
1 tablespoon cream

6 chicken breasts

2 large bags spinach leaves
3 cloves garlic, peeled and finely chopped
50g butter
nutmeg
salt and pepper
150ml cream

The fish should be skinned and boned, and cut into cubes. Put the fish into the bowl of a food processor and process until very smooth. Beat the egg in a bowl and add to the fish, along with the tarragon, salt and pepper, lemon juice and cream. Process again to a mousse-like consistency.

Slice each chicken breast down the length to make a pocket. Spoon the mousse into this pocket and fold to close. Chill for 20 minutes to set.

Put a frying pan on a high heat, then add the oil. Season the chicken and add to the pan. Cook until the chicken browns, turn, and add a little water. Cover the pan, turn the heat down and steam for 15 minutes.

Sauté the garlic in the butter and add the fresh spinach. Season with some grated nutmeg, salt and pepper, and finally stir in the cream.

Serve the chicken with a portion of the spinach.

This is my version of Surf and Turf, but I prefer to call it Surf and Chirp.

Sunday roast salmon with hollandaise

Serves 6

1 large turkey roasting bag

1 large side of salmon, filleted, skinned and boned

6 potatoes
thyme
olive oil
salt
3 carrots, peeled and sliced
3 parsnips, peeled and sliced
half a small turnip, peeled and diced
2-3 red onions, sliced
2 lemons

Hollandaise sauce
125g butter
1 teaspoon lemon juice
1 teaspoon vinegar
2 egg yolks
salt

Preheat the oven to 180ºC.

Slice the potatoes into 1cm slices. Toss them with thyme and olive oil and salt. Open the roasting bag and set a layer of potatoes in the bag. Season the salmon and place on top of the potatoes.

In a frying pan, sauté the carrots, parsnips and turnip over a high heat. Add the red onions and season with salt and pepper. Cook over a high heat until the vegetables begin to caramelise. Slice the two lemons and add them to the vegetables. Pour the whole lot into the bag on top of the salmon. Seal, and bake for 25 minutes.

To make the hollandaise: melt the butter over a medium heat. In a bowl, whisk together the lemon juice and vinegar and then add the egg yolks, whisking all the time. Stream in the melted butter, slowly whisking all the time as you do. Finally, add the salt.

Serve the salmon from the bag at the table, and pass the hollandaise sauce.

Try this as an alternative Sunday lunch dish: the salmon is roasted in a roasting bag, and the 'gravy' is a hollandaise sauce.

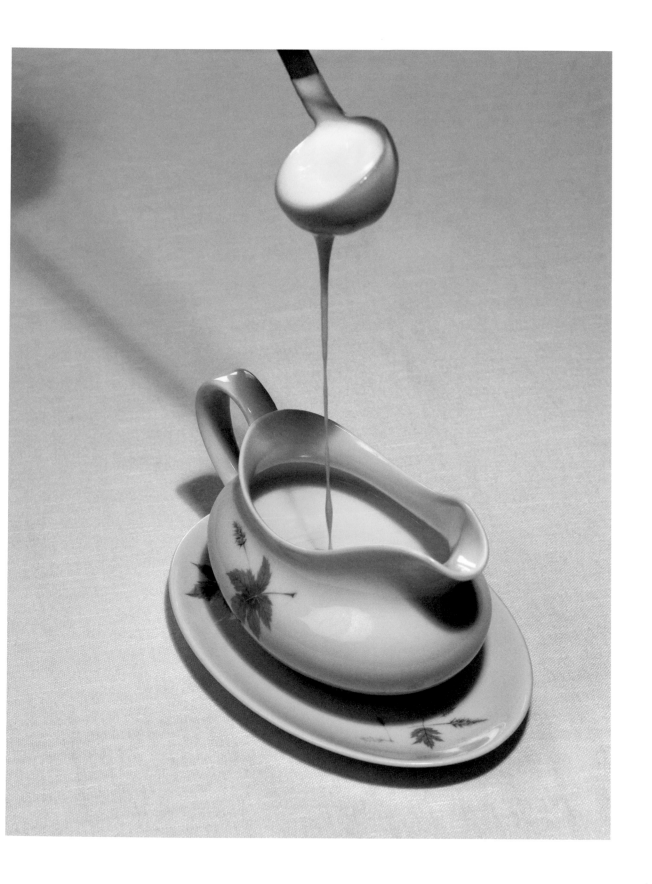

Salmon and cucumber wraps

Serves 4

half a cucumber, unpeeled
25ml white vinegar
2 tablespoons caster sugar
salt
handful of fresh dill, chopped
bunch of parsley
half a lemon, sliced
black peppercorns
1 centrepiece of fresh organic salmon (approximately 300g in weight)

Wasabi mayonnaise
150ml mayonnaise
3 tablespoons wasabi paste
bunch of wild rocket
8 flour tortillas
extra wasabi mayonnaise

If you have a mandolin, use this to slice the cucumber, otherwise slice it as thinly as possible with a sharp knife. Place the vinegar, caster sugar, salt and chopped fresh dill in a bowl and add the cucumber. Leave for about half an hour to marinate.

Put a pan of water on to boil and add the parsley, the slices of lemon, some whole black peppercorns and some salt, and into this simmering bouillon, add your salmon. Poach for approximately 10 minutes. Remove, cool and flake.

Make a wasabi mayonnaise by simply mixing the mayonnaise and wasabi together until smooth.

To assemble the wraps, spread each wrap with some wasabi mayonnaise, sprinkle over the cooled salmon flakes, then top with cucumber and rocket.

Roll up the wrap. You can serve them with more wasabi mayonnaise.

Its portability makes this a great alternative to a sandwich on a picnic and kids love them for school lunches. The secret extra deliciousness of flavour comes from the wasabi.

Trout with colcannon and mustard sauce

Serves 4

Colcannon
100g kale leaves
750g potatoes
150ml milk
3 spring onions, finely sliced
30g butter

Mustard sauce
200ml cream
50g butter
1 teaspoon English mustard
1 tablespoon grainy mustard
salt and pepper

4 trout fillets, skinned, pin bones removed
oil

Strip the kale leaves from the stalks and shred finely. Cook for a minute in a small amount of water. Peel, boil and mash the potatoes. Heat the milk and add to the mashed potatoes, stir in the kale and the spring onions and the butter.

Make the sauce by heating the cream and butter, and stirring in the two mustards.

Preheat your grill before you cook the trout. Brush a roasting tray with oil and put the empty tray under the grill to heat up. Take the tray from the grill and place the trout on top, turning the fish in the hot oil first to glaze. Grill the trout for about 8 minutes. There is no need to turn, because the hot tray will cook the underside of the fish.

When cooked, serve immediately with the colcannon, and drizzle with the sauce.

You can use a green cabbage for the colcannon if you don't have kale.

Salmon cakes with creamed leek

Makes 6 cakes

100g leeks, finely sliced and washed
50mls cream
25g butter
salt
juice of half a lemon
sprig of flat leaved parsley
250g organic fresh salmon
325g mashed potato
salt and pepper
seasoned flour
knob of butter

To make the creamed leek: heat the cream and butter, boiling to reduce slightly. Add the sliced leeks and cook very briefly (about 30 seconds). Remove from the heat.

Bring a small pot of water to a simmer and add salt, lemon and flat-leaved parsley. Poach the salmon in the simmering water until just cooked, allow to cool and then flake into pieces.

Gently mix together the fish, leeks and mashed potato. Wet your hands and form into six good-sized fishcakes. (You can also use an icecream scoop to help make portions, which then just need to be flattened slightly.)

Dip into seasoned flour, dust off the excess and place in the fridge to rest.

Cook exactly as you would a piece of fish, over a high heat for about 4 minutes per side. As you turn add a little butter.

Baked fillet of organic salmon with lime butter sauce

1 large side fillet of organic salmon
3 carrots
25g butter
juice of 1 orange
2 star anise
sea salt

Lime butter sauce
150ml cream
50g butter
juice of 2 limes
salt and pepper

Preheat the oven to 190°C.

Peel and thinly slice the carrots. Melt the butter in a frying pan and add the sliced carrots with the juice of the orange and the star anise. Cook for 2 minutes, then set aside to cool. Drain the carrots, but reserve the juices.

To make the lime butter sauce, bring the cream to the boil and simmer. Turn down the heat and add the butter and lime juice and season. Simmer for 4 — 5 minutes.

Place two sheets of kitchen foil three times the length of your salmon fillet on a worktop. Fold both in half. On to one sheet of foil, place half the thinly sliced carrots and place the salmon on top. Then layer the rest of the carrots on top of the salmon fillet, and place the star anise on top. Season with sea salt.

Place the second sheet of kitchen foil on top of the salmon, and begin to fold the sides up to make an envelope. After you have folded three sides and the fish is well enclosed, pour in the cooking juices from the carrot. Fold the final part of the foil, making sure everything is sealed.

Place the foil envelope on a baking tray and bake in the oven for 20 — 25 minutes. Open the parcel at the table and serve with the butter sauce.

Point-to-point salmon bap

4 escalopes of salmon, 100g each
4 soft bread rolls

Paprika mix
2 tablespoons paprika
1½ tablespoons ground cumin
1½ tablespoons ground coriander
salt and cracked black pepper

Tomato salsa
2 ripe tomatoes, roughly chopped
2 shallots, peeled and finely chopped
1 handful leaf coriander, chopped
juice of half a lime
1 teaspoon chilli sauce
pinch of salt

White cabbage salad
1 small head Dutch white cabbage (about 500g)
100ml white wine vinegar
1 teaspoon salt
1 tablespoon caraway seeds

Point-to-Point dressing
2 red peppers
olive oil
300ml mayonnaise
150ml white wine vinegar
30ml sugar
1 tablespoon pesto
1 clove garlic, minced
salt and papper

The white cabbage salad is best made the day before.
Very finely shred the cabbage using a mandolin or very
sharp knife. Stir in the vinegar, salt and the caraway
seeds, and leave overnight.

Make the tomato salsa by mixing the salsa ingredients
together in a bowl.

To make the dressing, preheat the oven to maximum.
Cut the peppers in half and remove their seeds.
Brush the skin with olive oil. Place on a hot tray in the
preheated oven and roast until the skin blackens (about
10 — 15 minutes). Take out of the oven and place in a
bowl, and cover with cling film. Cool for 10 minutes, and
then skin the peppers. Place all the dressing ingredients
into a blender and blend until sooth. Season to taste.

Coat each salmon escalope with the paprika mixture and
pat off the excess. Barbecue over a hot grill for two
minutes on each side.

To serve, slice the rolls, add the salmon, garnish with the
salad and the salsa, and drizzle over the dressing.

**Beef or salmon? We took these salmon baps to the Point to Point to compete with the
all too popular hamburger. We finished a respectable second.**

Darne of salmon with lazy man's hollandaise

Serves 2

Lazy man's hollandaise
2 tablespoons mayonnaise
juice of half a lemon
2 tablespoons lightly whipped cream

vegetable oil for cooking
400g salmon, cut into two darnes
Salt and pepper
fresh tarragon and lemon wedges to glaze

Mix together the mayonnaise (you can use a mayo from a jar), the lemon juice and the cream.

Preheat your grill.

Heat a pan until very hot, then when it is smoking add the oil. Season the salmon with salt and pepper and put the fish into the hot pan. Leave it there for about 2 — 3 minutes! Don't be tempted to move or turn it, you want a crust. Turn the fish over and cook for a further 2 minutes on the other side.

Put the fish onto your serving plates, and spoon over some of the sauce. Put each plate under a hot grill for a few seconds to give the sauce a toasty glaze.

Serve garnished with fresh tarragon and a wedge of lemon.

Ask your fishmonger to skin and bone the salmon, and then cut into darnes, thick slices, which cook quickly. I learned this sauce in the Butler Arms, and it's one for everybody's repertoire.

Round white fish

Firm, meaty, filling and full of flavour. Round white fish are adaptable, so if you can't get one fish for any of these recipes, don't think twice about swapping for another in the same family. The most famous of the round white fish is cod, but there are many other pretenders to its crown.

Thai-style white pollock fish cakes with Asian cabbage salad and a sweet and sour dipping sauce

Makes 8 fish cakes

450g pollock
3 spring onions
1 bunch coriander
1 red chilli
3cm root ginger
1 egg
juice of 1 lime
salt and pepper
sunflower or groundnut oil for cooking

Asian cabbage salad
half a Chinese cabbage
100g mange tout
1 large or 2 medium-sized carrots
juice of 1 lime
3 tablespoons sesame oil
generous handful of sesame seeds
salt and pepper

Sweet and sour dipping sauce
100ml apricot jam
25ml rice vinegar
juice of 1 lemon

Skin the pollock. Cut into chunks. Chop the spring onions and the coriander, and skin the ginger. Dice the chilli.

Blitz the fish for about 20 seconds in a food processor. Add the spring onion, coriander, chilli and grate in the fresh ginger. Crack the egg and whip lightly with a fork, add to the mix with the lime juice. Season.

Whiz everything to a paste in the food processor. Remove to a bowl and leave in the fridge for about 20 minutes to set, and for the flavours to fuse.

Meanwhile make the salad and the dipping sauce. Core the cabbage, removing the heart. Shred very finely. Top and tail the mange tout and cut into thin julienne strips. Grate the carrot. Toss the vegetables together, and add the lime juice and sesame oil. Toast the sesame seeds in a dry pan over a high heat for a minute, watching carefully that they don't burn, and add to the salad.

To make the dipping sauce, pour the three ingredients into a small saucepan and cook for two minutes, stirring, until the apricot dissolves and the three ingredients marry together.

To cook the fish cakes: using an ice-cream or potato scoop, or a large serving spoon, scoop out portions of the fish mixture. You should have enough for about eight fish cakes. Pat them down to make discs of about 2.5cm thick. It is very important to have a hot pan: when really hot add some sunflower oil, or groundnut oil. When smoking hot, add the fish cakes. Cook for 2 — 3 minutes per side and serve with the salad and the dipping sauce.

In France they pay more for pollock than for cod. This large-flaked fish is the fish of the future. It is very underrated here: I wonder is it the name that puts people off?

Roast cod with parsley mash

Serves 4

Parsley mash
20g parsley, chopped
50ml olive oil
8 — 10 potatoes, peeled
salt and pepper

4 portions of thickly cut fresh cod fillets
salt and pepper
2 tablespoons olive oil

Blend the parsley and olive oil in a food processor. Boil and mash the potatoes, whisk in the parsley oil and season.

Preheat the oven to its maximum temperature. Place an ovenproof pan on a high heat, and leave for 5 minutes until the pan is hot. Season the fish with salt and pepper. Add the olive oil to the pan; it should glisten and cover the base of the pan with a glossy film of very hot oil. Place the fish onto this searing heat, and cook for 2 — 3 minutes. Place the whole pan in the oven for a further 2 — 3 minutes until the fish is milky white and firm to the touch.

Serve with the parsley mash, and some tomato salsa.

As comforting as comfort food gets. You could substitute another fish from the cod family, including ling and white pollock. A lovely garnish for this dish is the tomato salsa on page 175.

Spiced haddock with couscous and courgettes

Serves 4

4 large fillets of haddock, skinned and boned
4 tablespoons taco seasoning
4 tablespoons plain flour
salt and pepper

Couscous and courgettes
250g couscous
4 tablespoons olive oil
500ml vegetable stock
pinch of saffron
1 small onion
1 courgette

crème fraîche
bunch of coriander

Place the couscous in a bowl and add a tablespoon of olive oil. Toss with a fork to coat the grains with the oil. Heat the stock with a good pinch of saffron. Turn the heat down and leave to infuse until the stock takes on the yellow colour of the saffron (10 — 15 minutes).

Finely dice the onion. Cut the courgette in four, length-ways, and then slice into 5mm-thick wedges. Put a pan on the heat and add 2 tablespoons olive oil. Add the onion and cook until it is just beginning to soften, and then add the courgette. Season quite generously with salt and pepper. Cook until the courgette is just soft. Add the vegetable mixture to the bowl of couscous. Bring the stock back to the boil and pour over the couscous mixture. Leave for 15 minutes for the grains to swell.

Mix the taco seasoning with the flour, and season.

To cook the fish: coat the haddock in the taco mix, pat to shake off the excess. Heat a pan and coat the base with vegetable oil. Cook the fish on a high heat for 4 minutes, turn and cook a further 4 minutes on the other side.

Serve with crème fraiche and chopped coriander.

This is a favourite with my family. Coating the haddock in a tasty taco seasoning mix is a great way for kids to learn to love fish.

Cod steaks with potato rösti and mushroom and leek sauce

Serves 4

Potato rösti
1kg potatoes
salt and pepper
small handful thyme leaves
vegetable oil for cooking

Leek and mushroom sauce
1 small onion
300g leeks
250g mushrooms
1 tablespoon vegetable oil
50g butter
50ml cream
salt and pepper
handful of chives, snipped to 1cm lengths

flour
salt and pepper
4 thick cod steaks
vegetable oil for cooking
knob of butter

To make the rösti, peel and grate the potatoes. Working in batches, place a quarter of the potato in the centre of a tea towel, collect the towel around it and squeeze hard to remove as much moisture as you can. Open out the towel and loosen the potato and season with salt and pepper and thyme. Repeat this process with the rest of the potato, but work quickly, because you don't want the potato to discolour.

Cook the rösti immediately. Heat oil in a frying pan, divide the potato mixture into four, and with each quarter spoon the potato into the centre of the pan and then press down to make a pancake-shaped rösti. Cook the rösti for 3 minutes on each side. It will come together and begin to crisp.

To make the sauce, chop the onion finely. Thinly slice the leeks and the mushrooms. Heat the oil in a sauté pan and cook the onion until it begins to soften. Add the leeks and the mushrooms, toss and cook until they soften, adding a little water if they get too dry. Add the butter. Cook for a minute and then add the cream. Taste and season. Add the chives.

When you are ready to serve, reheat the rösti and sauce. Put a pan on a high heat. Season the flour with salt and pepper, and dip the fish in the flour. Shake off the excess. Add some oil to coat the bottom of the pan and cook the fish for 3 — 4 minutes. Turn, add a knob of butter and cook 3 — 4 minutes on the other side. To serve, place the hot rösti on the plate, put the fish on top, and spoon over the sauce.

This dish is a great Saturday night staple, an alternative to steak with chips and onions. You can make the rösti in advance, and a lovely variation for the rösti is to add some grated carrot and courgette along with the potato, and you can substitute chives for the thyme leaves.

Pan-fried whiting with dilisk and lemon butter

Serves 4

4 fillets of whiting
flour
salt and pepper
vegetable oil for cooking
knob of butter

Dilisk and lemon butter
handful of dried dilisk
2 tablespoons lemon juice
the finely grated zest of half a lemon
125g salted butter

To make the butter: soak the dilisk for 10 minutes in warm water. Drain and chop finely. Then, using a pestle and mortar, blend the butter with the lemon juice and zest, then combine with the dilisk. Spoon onto a sheet of butter paper and roll up like a cracker. Chill for at least an hour in the fridge, or half an hour in the freezer.

Season the flour with salt and pepper. Dip the fish into the seasoned flour, shaking off the excess. Heat a pan on the stove and add the oil. Cook the fish for 3 — 4 minutes on a high heat. Turn over and add a knob of butter to the pan and cook the fish for another 3 — 4 minutes.

Cut the chilled dilisk and lemon butter into coin shapes, arrange on the hot fish and serve immediately.

Whiting is known as chicken of the sea, because of its sweet, open flavour. Ask your fishmonger to remove the pin bones.

Breaded fish fingers and tartare sauce

For each serving

200g white fish (cod, hake, haddock, large plaice fillets, whiting are all good)
flour, seasoned with salt and pepper
1 egg, beaten with a fork
white breadcrumbs
oil for frying

Tartare sauce
100ml mayonnaise
2 anchovies
1 tablespoon capers, chopped
4 gherkins, chopped
generous handful fresh parsley, chopped

Mix the ingredients for the tartare sauce together in a bowl.

Skin and debone the fish, and cut into finger-sized portions. Dry the fish carefully.

To make the breadcrumb crust, first dip the fish into the flour, dusting off any excess. Then dip in the beaten egg, once again removing any excess, and finally into the breadcrumbs.

To cook, deep or shallow fry until golden.

When we offered these fish fingers alongside a commercially made brand of fish fingers to Kinsale school kids, most of the children preferred the home-made. For kids of all ages, you can also serve this with tomato ketchup.

Poached hake with lemon butter sauce and champ

Serves 4

4 large hake fillets

Bouillon
bunch parsley
juice of half a lemon
salt
whole black peppercorns
500ml water

Champ
1kg potatoes, peeled
100ml milk
100g butter
3 spring onions

Lemon butter sauce
500ml cream
100g butter
juice of 2 lemons
salt and white pepper

Make a bouillon by adding 500ml water to a pan. Squeeze in the juice of half a lemon, add salt and whole black peppercorns. Bring to the boil, then turn down the heat to a simmer.

Cook the potatoes in salted water, drain, leave in the saucepan for a few minutes to dry. In a separate little pan, heat the milk and butter. Add the chopped spring onions. Add the warmed milk to the potatoes and mash lightly.

To make the lemon butter sauce, place all the sauce ingredients in a small pan and bring to the boil. Cook, stirring, until it reduces slightly.

When you are ready to serve, add the fish to the simmering bouillon. The fish will cook in just under 10 minutes. When it is ready, serve with a dollop of potatoes, and pour the sauce over.

An alternative way to poach the fish is to pour the bouillon into a deep roasting pan and poach in a 200°C oven for 10 — 12 minutes. This is a very controlled way to poach fish, and is especially suitable if you are cooking for large groups.

Pan-fried cod with salade niçoise and tapenade

Serves 6

Salade niçoise
1 clove garlic
10 cherry tomatoes
1 cucumber, peeled and thinly sliced
200g green beans, cooked
1 green pepper, seeded and sliced
1 small red onion, finely sliced
8 anchovy fillets, cut into pieces
1 heaped tablespoon capers
125g black olives
6 small new potatoes, cooked and cut in half

Niçoise dressing
90ml olive oil
2 tablespoons red wine vinegar
6 basil leaves, shredded

vegetable oil for cooking
6 cod steaks
flour, seasoned with salt and pepper
butter
jar of tapenade

Assemble the salad in a shallow bowl. First cut the garlic in half, and rub the bowl with the garlic. Arrange the salad ingredients attractively in the dish. Mix together the dressing ingredients and pour over the salad just before serving.

Heat a frying pan on a hot flame. Add some oil. Dip the cod steaks in the seasoned flour and place in the pan. Cook for 3 — 4 minutes, turn, add a knob of butter and cook for a further 3 — 4 minutes.

Serve the cod with the salad, and a spoonful of tapenade.

Southern France on a plate. Just remember to have that bottle of rosé wine nice and cool.

Fish and chips

Serves 4

8 potatoes
oil for deep frying
1 cup/130g plain white flour
4 tablespoons cornflour
salt and pepper
200ml sparkling water
750g of round white fish (cod, pollock, ling, hake)

First pre-cook the chips. Peel your potatoes and cut them into chip shapes. Heat the oil in a deep-fat fryer to 170°C. Pre-cook the chips in this oil, they are ready when they float, the insides are cooked, but they are still pale. You will crisp them later in hotter oil. Remove, dry on kitchen paper and set aside.

Make the batter by mixing the flour with the cornflour and seasoning with salt and pepper. Pour in the water, and beat until the mixture just comes together. You don't need to get rid of every lump, and overbeating will make your batter heavy.

Cut the fish into even-sized pieces. Don't make the pieces too large, because the fish will take too long to cook.

When you are ready to serve, heat the oil in the deep-fat fryer to 190°C. When the oil is up to temperature, dip each piece of fish in the batter and place into the hot oil. Using tongs, hold the fish suspended in the oil for half a minute to make sure it is sealed and won't stick to the bottom. Then cook for 6 — 8 minutes.

Take the fish out and immediately add the chips, which will cook in a couple of minutes at this high temperature. Serve at once.

The secret of this batter is the cornflour, which gives it crunch, and the sparkling water, which makes it light. If you're cooking fish and chips for a large number, you have no alternative but to make them a couple of portions at a time. Send them out while still hot and crunchy and move on to the next batch. It'll be worth the wait!

Warm chilli seafood salad

Serves 4

600g mixture of firm fish (salmon, gurnard, ray, prawns, scallops or monkfish)
flour, seasoned with salt and pepper
olive oil
3 tablespoons sweet chilli sauce
handful of fresh coriander, roughly chopped
spring onion, finely chopped
salad leaves

Red pepper dressing
2 red peppers
olive oil
300ml mayonnaise
150ml white wine vinegar
30ml sugar
1 tablespoon pesto
1 clove garlic, minced
salt and pepper

To make the dressing: Preheat the oven to maximum. Cut the peppers in half and remove their seeds. Brush the skin with olive oil. Place on a hot tray in the pre-heated oven and roast until the skin blackens (about 10 — 15 minutes). Take out of the oven and place in a bowl, and cover with cling film. Cool for 10 minutes and then skin the peppers. Place all the ingredients into a blender and blend until smooth. Season to taste.

Cut the fish into finger-sized slices. Dip the fish in seasoned flour and stir fry in hot oil, then add the sweet chilli sauce, coriander and spring onion, stirring gently to combine.

Toss the salad leaves in the red pepper dressing. Place the salad in a bowl with the warm fish on top.

I just can't take this off the menu at Fishy Fishy — it is one of our customers' absolute favourites. I like to serve it with crisp fried potato wedges and parsnip chips: we slice the parsnips using a potato peeler so that they are as thin as a crisp, and deep fry them in oil heated to 190°C. Make sure to use a firm fish and cut to an even size.

Fish barbecue

Salmon
Darnes of salmon, cut into small pieces so they cook quickly
Taco seasoning (page 108)
White cabbage and caraway salad (page 108)

Dip the salmon into the taco seasoning. Grill and serve on crusty bread with some of the cabbage salad.

Monkfish
Cut on the bias, diagonally, so that it cooks evenly
salt and pepper
vegetable oil
Asian butter sauce (page 173)

Season the fish and brush with oil. Barbecue and then drizzle with some of the warmed Asian butter sauce.

Tuna
Tuna steaks
Honey and soy glaze (page 170)

Cook the steaks for no more than 2 minutes per side, otherwise they will dry out. Pour over some of the glaze before serving.

Shellfish in their shells
Place oysters and scallops in the shells (drain the oysters, reserving the juice for another occasion) and place the shells on the fire. Wrap mussels and clams in an envelope of kitchen foil and put the foil on the fire. Any of the butter sauces in this book would work as a garnish.

Prawns
Cook the prawns in their shells, following the recipe on page 66. Place the cooked prawns on a platter and drizzle over with olive oil and pesto.

Why should steaks and sausages have command of our summer barbecues? Fish and shellfish is great for cooking outside on the fire, partly because it cooks so quickly. I've adapted some ideas from other recipes in this book, and from other recipes I've cooked at home to give some quick ideas on bringing seafood to the great outdoors.

Hake with fennel, orange and beetroot

Serves 2

Fennel and orange
1 fennel bulb
1 small onion
1 tablespoon cooking oil
handful of capers
knob of butter

Beetroot salsa
2 cooked beetroot
the juice of 1 orange
handful fresh mint, chopped
3 tablespoons Irish rapeseed oil (or olive oil)

2 fillets of hake, skinned

flour, seasoned with salt and pepper
rapeseed oil or vegetable oil for cooking

Cut the fennel in half, remove the heart and shred finely. Finely dice the onion. Heat a large frying pan and add the oil, cook the onion over a medium heat for a minute to soften, then add the fennel and a couple of tablespoons of water. Turn down the heat and simmer, partially covered, for 8 — 10 minutes. When it is cooked, add the capers and a knob of butter.

Cube the cooked beetroot and put in a bowl with the orange juice, mint and rapeseed oil.

Dip the fish in the seasoned flour. Tap off excess flour. Heat a frying pan and add some rapeseed oil. Fry the fish on a high heat for 3 — 4 minutes. Turn over and cook a further 3 — 4 minutes on the other side.

To finish the dish, put a spoonful of fennel on the plate, top with the fish, and garnish with the beetroot and a drizzle of rapeseed oil.

I like to use nutty, high-quality Irish rapeseed oil to make this dish — it brings out the earthy flavours of the beetroot and fennel. Rapeseed oil is great for cooking fish because it can stand very high temperatures.

Seafood crumble

Serves 6

Velouté sauce
1 litre fish stock
225ml cream
30g softened butter
30g flour

Crumble topping
bunch of fresh parsley
50ml olive oil
100g butter
150g breadcrumbs

1 tablespoon cooking oil
900g fresh white fish that has been skinned, boned and cut into uniform cubes (you can use haddock, salmon, monkfish, hake, as well as a few scallops and prawns for extra richness).

Preheat your oven to 170°C.

Make a velouté sauce by bringing the stock and cream to the boil. In a bowl, mix together the butter and the flour, and beat this roux, small piece by small piece, into the liquid. Stir over a medium heat, until the sauce thickens.

For the crumble topping, place the parsley into a blender and blend with the oil. Melt the butter for the breadcrumbs in a sauté pan, add the breadcrumbs and the parsley oil and stir to blend.

Put a frying pan on the heat and when hot, add the oil. Sauté the fish until just cooked. Pour the velouté sauce over the fish, mix together and pour into a casserole dish. Top with the breadcrumb mixture and cook for about 10 minutes in the preheated oven.

Fisherman's pie

Serves 4

Velouté sauce
1 litre fish stock
225ml cream
30g softened butter
30g flour
1 tablespoon mustard powder

Seafood mixture
900g fresh white fish that has been skinned, boned
and cut into cubes
150g leek
200g carrot

Potato topping
500g mashed potato
butter
Parmesan cheese, grated

Preheat the oven to 170°C.

Make a velouté sauce by bringing the stock and cream
to the boil. Mix together the butter and the flour, and beat
this roux, small piece by small piece, into the liquid. Stir
until the sauce thickens.

Steam the fish until just cooked. Grate the carrot, and
finely slice the leek.

Gently stir the fish and vegetables into the sauce and
pour into an oven-proof casserole, then top with a layer
of mashed potato. Dot with butter, and sprinkle over
grated Parmesan cheese. Bake in the oven for 15
minutes, until hot through, and golden.

Pan roasted hake with creamed parsnips and curry oil

Serves 4

Creamed parsnips
700g parsnips, peeled and quartered
50ml cream
2 tablespoons honey
25g butter
salt and pepper

Curry oil
200ml vegetable oil
1 teaspoon curry powder
pinch turmeric
pinch ground cumin

4 portions hake (approximately 200g each portion)
vegetable oil for cooking

Preheat your oven to 200°C.

To make the curry oil, mix the ingredients together in a small saucepan and simmer for 6 — 8 minutes. Let the mixture go cold before using.

Boil the parsnips in water until soft. Drain. Place the parsnips, 50ml of their cooking water, the cream, honey, butter and seasoning into the food processor, and process until smooth. (You can also use a hand held blender). Re-heat and season.

Use an ovenproof saucepan. Place the pan on a high heat, and when very hot add the oil. Cook the fish for 3 — 4 minutes, then place in the oven to finish, for a further 5 minutes.

To serve, place a spoonful of parsnip purée onto each hot plate and top with the fish. Drizzle curry oil all around the plate and serve.

Curry and parsnip is an anciently approved pairing, and it goes particularly well with fish.

Thai fish curry

Serves 4

1 onion, peeled and chopped
1 tablespoon vegetable oil
2 tablespoons yellow thai curry paste (you can also use red or green for a hotter curry)
1 can coconut milk
1 medium-sized carrot
1 medium-sized courgette
1 red pepper
1 small red onion
600g white fish (ling or pollock are recommended)
2 tablespoons vegetable oil
juice of 1 lime
a sprinkling of Thai fish sauce
lime juice and chopped coriander to serve

Cooked rice
2 cups Basmati rice
4 cups water
pinch of salt

Wash the rice carefully to remove the starch – you can do this in a sieve – until the water runs clear. Place in the pan, add four cups of water and the salt and place on a high heat with the lid off. Cook for approximately 10 minutes, after which the water will evaporate, forming potholes in the surface of the rice. When the water has all but disappeared, turn off the heat. Place a tea towel over the saucepan lid (this absorbs the steam) and cover tightly. Leave for 10 minutes, by which time the rice will be completely cooked, with each grain separate.

Sweat the onion in a tablespoon of vegetable oil. Add the curry paste and fry for 2 minutes. Add the coconut milk. Fill the empty can with water, and add the can of water. Simmer the sauce for about 15 minutes.

Carefully slice the vegetables into fine julienne strips. Skin, bone and dice the fish into cubes, about 3 cm square. If you have a wok, it is recommended to use this, otherwise a large frying pan will do. Heat the wok or pan, add the oil and then carefully stir fry the fish for a few minutes until coloured. Add the prepared vegetables and turn over for a few minutes in the pan. Add some lime juice and Thai fish sauce, and then pour in the coconut sauce. Cook for 3 — 4 more minutes, and then serve the curry sprinkled with more lime juice, and fresh coriander.

The lesser-known fish, such as ling and white pollock, are ideal for Thai currys. This is a great value family dish served with boiled rice.

Gurnard with glazed carrots, toasted pine nut and lime butter

Serves 4

700g carrots
60g butter
sugar

4 portions of gurnard (approx. 200g per portion)
flour, seasoned with salt and pepper
vegetable oil for cooking
large handful of pine nuts
the zest and juice of 2 limes
30g butter

Peel the carrots and slice on the diagonal. Melt the butter and sprinkle in a little bit of sugar. Add the carrots with a drop of water. Cook, uncovered for about 6 minutes until the carrots are tender and all the water has almost evaporated.

Dip the fish in the seasoned flour. Heat a pan until hot, add the oil and cook the fish for 3 — 4 minutes. Turn over and cook on the other side for the same length of time. Remove the fish to your warmed plates. Quickly add the pine nuts to the pan and let them toast. Add the lime zest and the butter. Squeeze in the lime juice and pour over the fish. Serve with the glazed carrots.

Gurnard is a fish that is becoming more and more popular due to its fantastic consistency and wonderful flavour. Contrary to popular belief, it is easy to remove the bones from gurnard. Ask you fishmonger to prepare it for you.

A little note when using limes: if you put the lime on the work surface and rub up and down, massaging the lime — you'll find you get a lot more juice out of it.

Casserole of gurnard and prawns

For each serving

Tarragon cream
700ml fish stock
250ml cream
1 onion, finely diced
30g butter
50ml white wine vinegar
25g flour
25g soft butter
1 handful fresh French tarragon, chopped

400g gurnard, cut into strips
400g prawns, peeled
1 tablespoon olive oil

To make the tarragon cream, boil together the fish stock and the cream until slightly thickened. In a separate pan sauté the onion in the butter. Add the white wine vinegar and boil until the vinegar has almost evaporated. Add the stock/cream mixture and heat again. Mix together the flour and soft butter. Have the creamy stock on a high simmer whilst you whisk in spoonfuls of this flour/butter mixture. The sauce will thicken into a smooth velouté. Add the chopped tarragon.

Preheat the oven to 200°C. If you have individual oven-proof casseroles, use these for this dish. Otherwise use just one large dish. Heat a pan to high heat, then sauté the fish in the olive oil for 2 minutes, then place the fish and prawns carefully into the casserole dish. Pour over the tarragon cream. The mixture should be quite saucy, with the pieces of fish sitting in a bath of the tarragon cream. Finish the casserole off in the oven for 4 — 5 minutes. Serve with boiled rice (see page 143).

We normally use red gurnard for this recipe, but equally good is grey gurnard – a sustainable, delicious-tasting fish that is becoming more and more popular. One of the secrets of this dish is the tarragon cream, where the vinegar sharpens the sauce, giving it a hint of acidity.

Smoked haddock risotto

Serves 4

1 onion, diced
2 tablespoons olive oil
300g Arborio risotto rice
1¼ litres chicken stock
1 cup cooked peas (fresh or frozen)
zest of 1 lemon
300g smoked haddock
1 tablespoon crème fraîche
salt and pepper
parsley or chervil

Sauté the onion in the olive oil until soft. Add the rice and stir until the rice is coated. Heat the chicken stock in another saucepan, and then add the stock to the rice, one ladleful at a time, stirring until the stock is absorbed between each ladle. When all the stock is absorbed, add the peas and the lemon zest.

Skin the haddock, and slice. Fold the fish into the risotto and let the risotto rest for a couple of minutes with the lid on. Finally stir in the crème fraîche. Season and scatter the parsley or chervil on top. Serve immediately.

There is no need to cook smoked haddock — you could slice it thinly and eat it like smoked salmon. So, when making this recipe add the fish at the very end, just to warm it.

Flat fish

These fish are delicate and rewarding to cook. Flat fish are delicious served on the bone, they roast and bake well, so these are adaptable friends for the cook.

Megrims on the bone, with lemon, anchovy, caper and dill sauce

For each serving

1 megrim, approximately 400g in weight
oil for cooking
salt

Anchovy butter
25g butter
2 anchovies, chopped
handful of capers
juice of half a lemon
handful of fresh dill

boiled new potatoes to serve

Ask your fishmonger to trim the fish by removing the head, and clipping the side fins off with a pair of sharp scissors. Leave the tail on.

Sprinkle an oven tray with oil. Place the fish on the tray, and drizzle the oil on top. Sprinkle over some salt and then grill on high for 6 — 8 minutes.

Make the butter sauce at the last minute (even after you've taken the fish out of the oven). Melt the butter, add the chopped anchovies, sprinkle in the capers and lemon juice. Sprinkle in the chopped dill and pour over the fish. Serve with boiled new potatoes.

Move over Dover sole. Megrim is the fish of the future. This is the fisherman's first choice to cook on the boat.

Baked fillets of plaice with parmesan and breadcrumb topping

Serves 2

25g butter
50g white breadcrumbs
25g Parmesan cheese
2 tablespoons crème fraiche
1 tablespoon mustard
2 tablespoons cooking oil
2 plaice, filleted into four fillets

Preheat the oven to 200°C.

Melt the butter and stir in the breadcrumbs. In a separate bowl, grate the cheese and stir in the crème fraiche and mustard.

Put a baking tray in the oven to heat. When it is hot, remove and add the oil, tipping the tray carefully to coat the bottom with hot oil.

Pat dry the plaice fillets with kitchen paper, place on the hot tray and season with salt and pepper. Spoon over the cream and cheese mixture, dividing evenly between each fillet. Top each fillet with a handful of buttered crumbs. Bake for 7 — 10 minutes in the oven, until the breadcrumbs are golden and the fish is cooked.

Plaice is at its best in the spring. You can easily tell if it's fresh when the orange dots that distinctively mark the skin are nice and bright.

This is a version of the classic technique, where the fillets are topped with a cheesy, breadcrumbed topping and then baked in the oven. Great with mash, and with fried potatoes, it's also an excellent and speedy lunch dish served with some brown soda bread.

Skate, black pepper and thyme fishcakes

Makes 6 cakes

250g skate, skinned and boned
325g mashed potato
fresh thyme leaves, chopped
crushed black pepper
salt
flour, seasoned with salt and pepper
vegetable oil for cooking

Steam the fish until just cooked, allow to cool and then flake into pieces. Gently mix together with the potato, thyme and black pepper. Season with salt.

Wet your hands, then form the mixture into fishcakes. You can also use an ice-cream scoop to portion them, and then simply press them flat. Dip the cakes in seasoned flour (dust off the excess). Place in the fridge to rest.

To cook, put a pan on the heat, and when it is hot add some cooking oil. Fry the fishcakes for approximately 4 minutes on each side.

The secret of these fishcakes is to keep the skate (or ray) in quite large pieces. The texture of skate has often been compared to that of chicken, and when it comes to fishcakes, this meatiness is a great advantage.

Ray with mussel sauce

Serves 2

4 fillets of ray (from 1 fish, you get 3 portions)
flour, seasoned with salt and pepper
vegetable oil for cooking
55g butter
1 onion, finely diced
10 mussels or cockles
75ml cream
juice of half a lemon

Ask your fishmonger to skin and bone the ray, and portion it for you. (One side of the ray yields two portions, the other side one.)

Dip the fish into seasoned flour. Heat a pan over a high heat until blazing hot, add a little cooking oil and sauté the fish for two minutes — you should hear it sizzle. Turn over, add a knob of butter and cook on the other side.

While the ray is cooking, prepare the shellfish sauce. Heat a pan on a medium heat, add the butter, and sweat the chopped onion for 2 minutes, until soft. Add the mussels (or cockles) and cream and a little lemon juice.

Arrange the fish on a serving plate, and pour the shellfish sauce over.

Ray, or skate, is the fish that is most closely associated with Dublin. But we shouldn't let Dubliners keep it to themselves. It's a fabulous fish, and this recipe works equally well with cockles.

Lemon sole with mango and cucumber salsa

Serves 4

4 fillets of lemon sole (skin on)
oil for cooking

Mango and cucumber salsa
1 mango
half a cucumber
6 sprigs of coriander
1 shallot, finely diced
juice of half a lime
1 teaspoon chilli sauce
pinch of salt

the juice of 1 lemon
3 tablespoons walnut oil
salt and pepper
mixed salad greens
handful of poppy seeds

To make the salsa: peel the mango and slice lengthways around the seed. Then dice into very small dice — the finer the better. Cube the unskinned cucumber into very fine dice as well. Shred the coriander. Put all the salsa ingredients into a small bowl and stir to combine.

Make the salad dressing by mixing together the lemon juice, walnut oil, salt and pepper. Toss the salad leaves in the dressing, and add the poppy seeds.

Heat a pan until very hot. Add some cooking oil and cook the fish, flesh side down first, for approximately three minutes. Turn and cook for three minutes on the other side.

Divide the dressed salad between four plates, top with the fish and serve with the salsa.

When you are chopping herbs and garlic, don't over chop. I always say, keep the flavour in the herb, not on the board. This is a bright, light, summer recipe. Leave the skin on for this one, because it helps to cook the sole evenly.

Prime fish

These meaty specimens are prized by chefs, but their cooking can also be simple and homely.

John dory with asparagus

Serves 2

10 spears of asparagus
pinch of sugar
knob of butter
salt

Sun-dried tomato and oregano sauce
50g semi-sundried tomatoes
30g butter
zest of 1 lemon
handful of fresh oregano, chopped

4 fillets of john dory (skin on)
flour, seasoned with salt and pepper
vegetable oil for cooking

Break the tips off the asparagus and boil in a little water that has a little sugar, butter and salt in it.

To make the sauce: chop the tomatoes into large chunks. Melt the butter and add the tomatoes to the butter with the lemon zest and the oregano.

Dip the fish in seasoned flour, and pat off the excess. Heat the pan to very hot and then add some oil. Place the fillets skin side down on the pan, and fry the fish for 4 minutes, then turn and cook the other side for a further 4 minutes.

Put the asparagus on a plate. Top with the fish and pour the sauce over.

I call dory the 'keep fit fish', because of its ultra-active swimming style. This recipe uses just the tips of asparagus; use the remaining asparagus stalks for soups or salads.

Pan-fried brill with courgettes and basil

Serves 4

450g courgettes
1 small onion
2 cloves garlic
2 tablespoons olive oil
salt and pepper
100g semi-sundried tomatoes
75ml cream
knob of butter
juice of half a lemon
handful of chopped fresh basil leaves

4 fillets of brill, boned and skinned
flour, seasoned with salt and pepper
oil for cooking the fish
knob of butter

Cut the courgettes in half, lengthways, and then slice into half moons, about 5mm thick. Peel and dice the onion, and slice the garlic.

Heat a pan over medium heat and add 2 tablespoons olive oil. Add the onion and garlic and sauté a couple of minutes until beginning to soften. Add the courgettes, season with salt and pepper, and cook until they too begin to soften. Add the tomatoes, the cream, butter and lemon juice.

Dip the brill fillets into seasoned flour and dust off the excess. Heat a pan over a high heat, add some cooking oil. Fry the brill for 4 minutes, then turn, add a knob of butter and fry on the other side for a further 4 minutes.

Just before serving, stir some fresh basil into the courgette stew, and serve with the fish.

Whole crisp-fried sea bream with pineapple salsa

Serves 2

Pineapple salsa
half a pineapple
half a cucumber
6 sprigs of coriander
1 shallot, finely diced
juice of half a lime
1 teaspoon chilli sauce
pinch of salt

2 whole sea bream
flour, seasoned with salt and pepper

4cm fresh ginger, peeled and cut into julienne strips
2 spring onions, shredded
toasted sesame oil
handful of white and black sesame seeds, toasted

To make the salsa: peel the pineapple with a knife, and dice, as small as you can, into very small dice — the finer the better. Cube the unskinned cucumber into very fine dice as well. Shred the coriander. Put all the salsa ingredients into a small bowl and stir to combine.

Before cooking, score both sides of the fish with three slashes. Roll the fish in seasoned flour and pat off the excess.

Preheat the deep-fat fryer to 180°C and place the fish in the hot oil. Turn up the heat and cook at 190°C for about 8 — 10 minutes, until the fish is crispy.

Drain the fish on kitchen paper, and then place on a hot platter. Sprinkle over the strips of ginger and spring onion, and drizzle with the sesame oil. Finally scatter over some toasted sesame seeds and serve with salsa on the side.

This recipe is inspired by the way fish is often served in Asian restaurants: deep-fried whole, so that it is crispy on the outside. This technique means that it is steamed and moist within. Ask your fishmonger to gut and scale the fish, and cut off the fins with scissors. To eat the fish, just lift the flesh away from the bone. This is very informal food.

Seared tuna steak

Serves 4

Honey and soy dressing
100ml soy sauce
100ml toasted sesame oil
50ml white wine vinegar
100ml honey
½ clove garlic, minced

4 tuna steaks (approximately 200g each)
olive oil

a small bowl full of herb salad (including coriander,
chervil, flat leaf parsley and chives)
2 spring onions, finely sliced
1 red chilli, finely sliced
the juice of half a lemon
2 tablespoons olive oil
salt and pepper
toasted sesame seeds

Place all the ingredients for the honey and soy dressing in a small pan and bring to the boil. Boil until the sauce is reduced and thickened (it should coat the back of a spoon). Reserve while you cook the tuna.

Brush the tuna steaks with olive oil and grill or barbecue over a high heat for about 2 minutes per side. Don't overcook, or they will become dry.

Toss the salad leaves, spring onions and chilli in the lemon juice and olive oil, and season.

Serve the tuna topped with some honey and soy dressing, a handful of dressed herb salad and, finally, some toasted sesame seeds.

Monkfish with Asian butter sauce

Serves 2

Asian butter sauce
125g butter
2 tablespoons sweet chilli sauce
2.5cm ginger, peeled and cut into julienned slivers
2 spring onions, shredded
1 bunch coriander, roughly chopped

2 fillets of monkfish (approximately 200g per portion)
vegetable oil for cooking
cooked basmati rice for serving

Make the Asian butter sauce: melt the butter and add the rest of the sauce ingredients, stirring to combine.

Cut the monkfish into even slices, cut on the bias — at a slight diagonal. This will help it to cook evenly.

Heat a pan over a high heat and add some oil. Season the fish and cook in the hot oil for 2 minutes on each side.

Serve the monkfish on a bed of cooked basmati rice and drizzle the butter sauce over.

The most important thing about monkfish is to take off his 'vest' — that's the inner coating of skin that lies under its outer skin. It comes off with a sharp knife — your fishmonger will do this for you if you ask him.

Sea bass with buttered leeks and tomato salsa

Serves 4

Tomato salsa
2 ripe tomatoes
1 shallot
1 handful leaf coriander
juice of half a lime
1 teaspoon sweet chilli sauce
pinch of salt

Buttered leeks
300g leeks
1 tablespoon vegetable oil
50g butter

flour, seasoned with salt and pepper
4 fillets of sea bass, each approximately 180g in weight
vegetable oil for cooking

Slice the tomatoes in half, horizontally and remove the seeds. Finely dice the flesh of the tomato. Dice the shallot and shred the coriander. Place all the ingredients in a bowl and stir gently to combine. Place in the fridge for 30 minutes before serving.

Thinly slice the leeks. Heat the oil and butter in a saute pan and cook the leeks until they begin to soften.

Heat a pan to a very high heat, add some cooking oil. Dip the fish fillets into the seasoned flour, pat off the excess, and cook for four minutes. Turn and cook the other side for three to four minutes. Serve with the buttered leeks, ganished with the tomato salsa.

I love this tomato salsa, it goes so well with so many fish preparations, and we find using the sweet chilli sauce, rather than fresh chilli, controls the temperature, giving the salsa a fresh, piquant hit that will compliment and enliven your cooking.

Penne pasta with tuna in tomato sauce

Serves 2

1 onion, finely chopped
1 clove garlic, sliced
2 tablespoons vegetable oil
425g can whole plum tomatoes
1 tablespoon tomato paste
salt and sugar to season

250g fresh tuna
vegetable oil for cooking
salt and pepper
200g penne pasta
handful each of black olives and capers
basil

Put the pan on the heat over a medium heat, add the oil, the onion and garlic and cook until softened. Chop the tomatoes roughtly — you don't want the sauce too smooth. Add the tomatoes to the softened onion and then add the juice. Add a tablespoon of tomato paste. Add a splash of water. Cook for 15 — 20 minutes. Season with salt and sugar.

To prepare the tuna, cut into finger strips. Put another pan on the heat, and when very hot add some oil. Season the tuna and place in the hot pan. Cook briefly, tossing in the oil, for just a couple of minutes.

Cook the pasta in boiling water, and drain. Add the capers and olives to the tuna, and then the tomato sauce. Toss with the cooked pasta and serve garnished with the basil.

You can use fresh tomatoes for this but, if you do, skin them first before adding to the sauce.

Dover sole on the bone with drawn butter

For each serving

1 Dover sole (approximately 500g in size)
flour, seasoned with salt and pepper
olive oil
75g butter
lemon wedges

Ask your fishmonger to skin the sole, and remove the head and fins, but leave the tail.

Preheat the oven to 220°C.

Roll the fish in the seasoned flour, pat off the excess. Drizzle some olive oil on an oven tray and place the tray in the hot oven. When the tray is hot, remove from the oven and, quickly rolling the fish in the olive oil first, place the sole on the tray and roast for 6 — 8 minutes.

To make the drawn butter, put a ramekin of butter into the microwave for 30 seconds to melt (use a saucepan on the heat, if you don't have a microwave).

Serve the fish with a little pot of drawn butter and the lemon wedges.

They say, of sole, that they have one eye looking at you, and one eye looking for you.

John dory with roast fennel

For each serving

1 john dory per person (approx 350g in size)
1 fennel bulb per person
vegetable oil for cooking
50ml vegetable stock
sea salt
thyme
two slices of lemon
oil

The john dory should be whole, on the bone, with head and tail removed, and the side fins cut off with scissors. Score three deep cuts into one side of the fish. John dory has no scales so you can eat the skin.

Preheat the oven to 200°C.

Cut the fennel in half, then in quarters. Carefully leave a little bit of the heart in the centre of the bulb to hold it together. Put an ovenproof pan on the heat, and add a little oil. Cook the fennel on a high heat to give it a good colour and bring out the flavour. Add the stock and place in the oven for 8 minutes.

Put a baking tray in the oven to heat up for a few minutes. Press some sea salt and thyme into the three slashes in the fish, and insert two slcies of lemon in the centre of the fish. Drizzle some oil over the hot tray and place the fish on top. Brush with oil and cook for 12 minutes. Serve with the roast fennel.

Index

Index

Index

Index

Index

Design Carla Benedetti
Copy Editor Judith Casey
Editor Sally McKenna
Publishing Editor John McKenna
Food Styling Sally McKenna

A note on the type

The body text of this book is set in Helvetica 9pt on 13pt.
The masthead and ingredients text are set in AFBattersea.

Printed in Spain by GraphyCems